QUITTING WORK TO START A BUSINESS

IN 2016

$ $

$ $

FROM A SIX FIGURE ENTREPRENEUR

WHO DID EXACTLY THAT

Bonus! - As a way of saying thanks, here's a short book that is guaranteed to excel your business career. It helped me greatly and will do the same for you if you can internalise the concepts.

Download Here → *http://goo.gl/iYx5aC*

QUTTING WORK TO START A BUSINESS IN 2016

From a SIX Figure Entrepreneur who did Exactly That

Written By:

Mateen S

Brought to you by AffEngineer.com

www.AffEngineer.com Copyright © 2015 by AffEngineer Publishing

Disclaimer

No part of this publication may be reproduced or transmitted in any form or by any means, mechanical or electronic, including photocopying or recording, or by any information storage and retrieval system, or transmitted by email without permission in writing from the publisher.

While all attempts have been made to verify the information provided in this publication, neither the author nor the publisher assumes any responsibility for errors, omissions or contrary interpretations of the subject matter herein.

This book is for entertainment purposes only. The views expressed are those of the author alone, and should not be taken as expert instruction or commands. The reader is responsible for his or her own actions.

Adherence to all applicable laws and regulations, including international, federal, state and local laws governing professional licensing, business practices, advertising and all other aspects of doing business in the US, Canada or any other jurisdiction is the sole responsibility of the purchaser or reader.

Neither the author nor the publisher assumes any responsibility or liability whatsoever on the behalf of the purchaser or reader of these materials.

Any perceived slight of any individual or organization is purely unintentional.

Introduction

Life can go by real quick if you let it. The quickest 2 years of my life were when I was employed full-time as a university graduate. It was during these years I made a conscious decision to not allow myself to get caught up in the 9-5 grind.

Many of us realise after a couple years into our career that we are destined for a lot more. That we're meant to be doing something else and after sometime the inability or lack of time we have to work on our ideas begin to frustrate us.

This is what happened to me. I went through many different phases until I pulled the plug on work and decided to never look back no matter how bad my situation got. It made me desperate to make business work and I've never regretted the decision.

This book is going to be a mixture of the whole experience. From my journey to my current 6 figure business to issues you'll face if you make the decision and how to overcome them.

I write it as a friend to another friend and even though I probably don't know you personally, I know what you're going through and can relate to your frustrations.

Table of Contents

My Story From Work Slave to Entrepreneur

Beginnings

I've always been the business type. Selling things at school, selling things at university and looking out for business opportunities at my workplace.

When we'd play family videos, I'd be playing 'buy and sell' with my toy cars and have recordings of myself trying to sell them for a million dollars to my dad who bought them for $2. They were Ferrari toy cars if that makes it less sad. Looking back at these videos now makes me realise how much entrepreneurship was ingrained in me and how much it's probably ingrained in most entrepreneurs. It's not just something that pops up in my head from time to time, it's something that dominates my thoughts when I'm in the house, when I'm out shopping, when I'm hanging with friends.

Hardly anyone I hung around thought this way. Almost none were fascinated by my breakdowns of how much a certain business idea could be making and I later realised I was probably boring them with all this talk.

I'd get excited at the thought of trying a certain business out while my friends would just shrug it off as if it was uninteresting. Maybe it was, to them, but for me, business was fascinating. Making money out of nothing was like magic.

I went to school like everyone else and although there was a business side of me somewhere in there, I had to hide it away to make sure I got good grades and consequently make my parents proud.

I listened and did well at school. I did what I thought was the right way to live my life, listening to our elders since they're the more experienced humans. Life was like a big robot world where if you just did something a certain way, you'll be happy. This is how I thought.

'Business me made an appearance here and there at school. I'd invest my part time income into buying things on eBay or Gumtree and trying to sell them at a higher price.

During Uni, I invested 10k into the stock market just to see how it all worked. I made some money and was happy but again, I had to hide my inclines so that I could pass my subjects and get good grades.

Full-Time Work

I finally got a job at a Civil Engineering firm. A career I had worked 4 years of my life to get into was becoming a reality. It was the largest construction firm in Australia so I felt like I was doing everything right. Everyone was congratulating me and were in awe of what I had achieved.

My family were proud to tell my extended family what I'm doing. My friends and I were considered 'successful', 'smart', 'bright' and every other motivating term in the book. I must have been doing it all right I thought to myself.

I started earning a great salary and made great intelligent friends. I made awesome contacts with people around the industry. I felt I was an up and coming engineer and felt I would have a successful career in Construction as long as I continued.

This was awesome for the first year. I was being challenged and learning new things every day. I was put in charge of small projects and made to hold important meetings. I implemented growth strategies, went to construction sites to tell people what to do. It felt good. It felt like I had fast-tracked myself to where a lot of people dreamed of being.

Inklings

Then slowly, 'Business me', started to resurface. I'm naturally a good saver and put the majority of my money straight into the bank. As my bank account grew, my mind would begin wondering how I can make my money work for me. I read Rich Dad Poor Dad and this made these feelings grow even stronger.

As months went by, I started to slack at work. I used to happily bring my work home to study so I can perform my job better. I'd make a conscious effort to network with people. I'd make sure I was on top of my tasks and could offer help to my peers. Not anymore. It was the opposite.

Now I avoided my work phone. Work that needed to be done at home annoyed and frustrated me and I'd get hassled constantly for work I should have gotten done days ago. In my industry, falling behind can really bite you in the behind. People depend on me so that work flows smoothly. A small delay in permit acquisitions can put projects days behind costing people hundreds, sometimes thousands. People get real upset if I'm not doing my job right.

I didn't care about all this. Well I did, a little, but for the most part, I really didn't care. I'd do the bare minimum at work and spend most of my time looking into franchises that I could afford.

Can't Take it Anymore

It finally came to a point where I couldn't be there anymore. Every day there was torture and while my actions had to be work related, my mind was in a totally different space. The only fun part about work was talking to my colleagues about all the fun stuff they got up to, the rest was a bore.

It's not that the work was unexciting. There was always something new everyday and it challenged me to grow, it's more that my lack of focus made it all feel like I _had_ to do it, not something I had a choice over.

I started seriously looking into franchises at this stage. I looked into buying into telco firms and started booking myself in with business development managers at these firms to look at franchisee models.

I saved enough to get into one. I spent 2 months getting a business plan together, a team together, setting up the legal documentation and was a couple weeks away from opening this new franchise. I decided to quit work so I could have few days to relax before I start with this new venture. To new beginnings. Two weeks, and I'll finally be able to do something that I like. I won't have to hide the 'Business me' anymore. I can finally explore the business world not feeling guilty.

Business Life Starts

Two weeks went by and I received a call from my Franchisor. Their division had been cut and the franchisee – franchisor model was taken out of their company.

What did this mean for me? My contract was now void and it was no longer a possibility to have my own franchise anymore. I was now unemployed with absolutely no plan. Most people would have been scared. Most people would have probably gone back to work but I started to think that it was all gods plan of giving me that push to actually quit work.

I felt like it was a good thing. I now had all this time and a decent experimental budget to try business for a couple years. If I lived off of my savings and limited my expenses, I could live a cool 2 years at home experimenting a bunch of different things and if it still didn't work out, I'd happily go back to work. At least I could tell myself I tried.

This is where it all began. The real journey of entrepreneurship.

Business Idea After Business Idea

Business is hard to get rolling. I mean, it's easy to read case studies here and there and feel like you can do it to but to put it all into action for a sustained period of time is a difficult task.

At the start of my journey I was still stuck in a workers mindset. It had been drilled into me for years so reseting myself was a challenge. If you've been in business full-time for more than a year, you'll know what I'm talking about.

There are certain habits and mindset changes you need to incorporate before you start getting anywhere with business. Some are big, some are small, but they're all important.

At the start of my journey it became apparent that I had a lot to learn. Every business idea I tried seemed to flop hard. I'd start something with the hopes of it becoming huge and then be disappointed with the results upon launching. From yard sale hunting to blogging to making phone apps, it was all the same. I'd have a product I'd have worked on for weeks, sometimes months but I couldn't get anyone to buy/download it. Why? What was I missing?

This continued for 6 months. Business idea after business idea, I was working on a new one every week. People started to laugh when I'd tell them a new idea I had. I had no idea if it was the right or wrong thing to do but every new idea I'd get, it would make the previous idea feel mediocre.

That's until I realised a couple of simple truths. Any business that makes people money needs marketing and any business that's going to bring in an income requires a certain time commitment before ditching it for another idea.

Six months down the track I stumbled upon paid affiliate marketing. The idea of bringing companies more business and getting paid out referral commission. I can make money and learn marketing at the same time.

I knew I had to make this work no matter what. I needed to learn good marketing and this seemed like the best way. Instead of spending all that time building a business and then marketing it. I could simply go to websites like Shareasale, Amazon, Maxbounty and search through a database of companies that would accept affiliate marketers.

That's when I decided to stick to this no matter what. No matter how long it took, I was going to make it work. I decided to ditch my back up plan. "I'm not going to work no matter what". Even if I'm on the streets begging, I'm going to make it work. I didn't care about anything anymore. It was as if nothing else in the world mattered except for affiliate marketing. My mind would immediately shut down new ideas and I'd happily spend 12 hours a day trying to crack this affiliate marketing thing.

Importance of Marketing

Marketing is everything. No idea is good unless it is in front of its target demographic. There's no point working on something if you have no idea how to get interested people to buy/engage with it.

Every successful business has to continuously engage in marketing efforts to maintain it's position and to grow further.

This is the part that took me 6 months to realise. It was definitely a long learning curve, but I got there. If you haven't done much business yet, remember this,

"If you don't have an idea of *how* you're going to get people to buy your product – don't do it."

Most people, including I, did things the wrong way. I would spend weeks, months building something and then would look for buyers. Real businessmen do things the opposite way. They look for buyers and interest before they even start their product. In business, it's called 'product validation'.

Product validation isn't a new concept, it's a frame of thinking you need to get used to if you want to really make money in business. Instead of wasting all this time working on something and then figuring out it's a bad idea, why not try and learn this out straight away? Why not run a small test and see if there is enough interest for you to make money with?

At the end of the day, business comes down to someone pulling out their wallet and making a purchase. If you can't get someone to do this, then it's a bad business idea.

This was a realisation I had one day that settled right into the core of my business process. It was stuck with me. I wasn't willing to work on any business idea until I had validated it. Till I could prove to myself that someone was willing to make a purchase.

Oh, and when validating, don't ask your friends or family if they'd 'buy' it. Of course, they want you to feel good and will end up giving you an answer that won't break your heart.

Even if you have honest people in your circle that tell you how it is, whether it's a good idea or a bad idea, still try get someone not connected to you to buy your product or service. There's a big difference between saying, 'I would buy that', and actually going through with a purchase.

Breakthrough - Focus

Things took a turn for me once I realised the importance of marketing. I was now learning how to drive Google and FaceBook traffic straight to products/services and seeing if they converted into a purchase. I was learning what makes people purchase online, what landing pages convert better, key words that sell, good niches where money can be made, this was business.

It took me 19 gruelling 12 hour days in this business to make my first sale of $5.25. It was for a cloud service that paid $5.25 per person you could get to sign up with them.

I was over the moon. I had paid about $20 for marketing to make that sale but it was still a breakthrough. It was the first time I had made proper money on the internet and I had felt like I had done something no one in my circle thought was possible. At that point, I felt like I was going to be alright. That I had made the right choice. Six months after I quit my job I finally made some money. It took a lot longer than I thought but it happened and it was great.

Sales started to become more frequent and after a few months I was making $1-$2k profit per month. It went from just wanting to make enough to survive to actually wanting to make the same money as I did when I was working full-time which was about $50k after taxes.

As I continued, I got better and started hitting some huge numbers. I'd have days where I'd make $500, days I'd make $1,000 and days I'd even make $7,000 in profit! It was crazy. There weren't many of those days, but when they happened it pumped my bank account right up.

Online selling has limitless potential. You can be selling things to people in Sweden, people in Jamaica, people in New Zealand. To people you've never met before. The online world has connected money between people from all over the world so if you have a hot product selling somewhere online, with the right type of marketing, you can get this product in front of all the potential customers in the online world and when that happens, you make a LOT of money.

This is why phone apps can make people millions. It's why Amazon is a multibillion dollar company and it's why some people are so obsessed in getting something to work for them online.

Building my Empire

As time progressed I diversified my business. I sold a variety of merchandise from custom hoodies to custom shoes. I sold services, I sold forum subscriptions, I sold anything that would make me a positive return after advertising costs.

I was, (and still am), an online marketer. Someone that finds where and how to pay for advertising that brings in customers that buy.

My blog became more and more popular as I wrote about my income and how I made what I made. I blogged all my tips and tricks. I made youtube tutorials that brought in a tonne of traffic. Eventually my blog started to make me more money than my marketing business! I started to leverage my success to other businesses and build my brand, my name and consequently my income.

Business is a funny thing. Success breeds more success. It makes you feel like mentally you can get to where you want to be. If you earn $5, it will give you the confidence that you can earn $50. If you earn $50, you feel like you can earn $500. People love hearing about how you made this happen so will visit our blog, keep up to date with your progress and will purchase things you recommend them, (with honesty of course).

If you have success with your business, you can build a blog, write a book, make a forum, mentor people and expand in ways you never thought possible. Many entrepreneurs make a huge amount of money just selling energy. They do talks and seminars and motivate people about how they made things happen.

The Realities of Business

Business today has become a whole different beast from when I first started. I used to think it was easy, that I could get there doing what I was doing even though I wasn't doing much.

Business is tough. It requires a tonne of persistence. Time after time you'll fail and will be let down by the way things turn out. The difference between someone that makes it and someone that doesn't is that successful people will continue going. They may feel demotivated, they may doubt their decisions 100 times over, they might even take a short break from time to time _but_ they continue making progress. Even small things, compounded over time will start to add up.

Business is mean. You might think you have an idea that will change the world. The amount of times I've been emailed to help someone with their guaranteed 'million dollar idea' is too many. The world doesn't care how you feel about your idea. That you've spend days, months, years planning it, thinking about it, strategising, networking, etc.

No matter how good you think your idea is, put it to the test in the real world. Put up a simple landing page on a website and drive traffic to it. See how people react. Do they sign up? Do they buy things? Do they spend 5 seconds on your site and go somewhere else? Real data never lies and no idea is a 'million dollar idea' until it's actually makes you a million dollars.

Business for me today has become a lot of the above. Just chugging along, sticking to what I've found to work and ideas I like experimenting with. This book is an experiment. It's one of my first kindle books. I'm intrigued with how popular kindle is getting and instead of just thinking about it I spend a month listing topics and pumping out 5 test books I'm putting up soon. Let's see how they go!

The Challenges You'll Face

There are so many challenges that come with the transition from work to entrepreneurship. I'm going to list the important once below so you can be prepared.

Managing Your Spare Time

Your 8-10 mandatory working hours are no more. There is so much to do and so many fun ways you could be spending your time. You could be playing games, going to the beach, seeing friends, sleeping, doing everything you dreamed of while at work.

It's true, you _can_ do all these and you should on your break days but on working days you _work_. Business doesn't happen by itself. You have to make it happen. Every successful business man or woman who's enjoying life travelling the world worked very hard to get to where they did. They worked harder than when employed. Many lived out of their car to cut costs and to have money to put back in their business. They cried, they doubted, they hustled it out. They did what was necessary to make it work.

Be careful with what you fill all this spare time with. It's good to be healthy and exercise and all but don't fill up all this time with a lot of unnecessary things. Too much play time will put you on the wrong road to business, if you can even call it that.

Business comes first. You need to work hard to make a break through so lock yourself in your room, turn off all social media and distractions and get to work!

Distractions

Talking about distractions there are an abundance of those these days. From phone apps to people calling and pestering you for your time, it just never ends.

I've written a book about Productivity Mastery. It's one of my best books and goes through a bunch of different strategies I employ to make sure I get my work done.

When I work, I turn my phone on silent and put it upside down so I can't get distracted with notifications and messages. I close all non-work related windows and internet browser tabs. No music, no documentaries or things playing in the background, just solid, uninterrupted work.

You see, work momentum is a concept you're probably familiar with. When you've been working on something for more than 20 minutes, you're whole body and mind will have optimised itself to focus in on the activity. Turning your attention to something else will reset this momentum and put you out of your zone. Keep yourself in it. Keep your self working at optimum pace for as long as you can. _This_ is why I don't let myself get distracted.

When you work, you work. Even 4 straight hours of uninterrupted work is a lot of work compared to someone who works on and off at a 8 hour desk job.

Money

You now, don't have a job, or maybe you have a part-time one which is great but right now, more than any other time in your life you need to be spending your money wisely.

I had a limited bank account and no income. Every dollar I spent was one dollar closer to going back to work if I couldn't make this work. Don't spend money on stupid things. Cut down as much as you can. I just spent money on food, living and a bit of leisure. You won't survive long if you have a hard time saving and you're living on a budget.

Business people know how to manage their finances. There's not a single successful businessmen who doesn't know how to save. It's fundamental to your success. You'll have too many opportunities pass you by because you didn't have money at the time. Don't be that person.

If you have cashflow coming in, that's great, if you don't, and have just a bank account, make sure you're learning with every dollar spent.

Motivation

Motivation is a funny thing. It comes and goes as it pleases. There would be days I'll have tonnes of motivation and would jump out of bed at 5am ready to get straight into work. The very next day I'd question why I'm doing all this.

You will need to learn how to switch yourself in and out of what I like to call 'robot mode'. When you have little motivation but still need to get things done, this is what makes or breaks a true entrepreneur.

You need to be able to keep going, keep moving forward no matter what. You don't always have to work 10 hour days. If you can manage 2 hours and it's a better choice for your sanity then do that but make sure it's consistent.

Every entrepreneur fell in and out of motivation. It's normal. If you can get yourself to keep moving forward even when you really don't want to, then it'll come back. Make it a point to always finish your projects before ditching them. It's easy to stop something and move to something more exciting but if you do this over and over again you'll achieve nothing.

Many of my hobbies and entrepreneurship activities that are now in a more stable routine have come from me forcing myself to get started with.

Take boxing for example. I've liked the sport of boxing for a long time. I love following famous personalities and keeping up with boxing news. I've also wanted to start boxing as an amateur for a while and after dwelling on the idea for a long time I decided to just join a boxing gym and get consistent with going there first. At first, I had to force myself to go there for the first 2 weeks. It was tough. Yes, I enjoyed it but almost everyone would much rather be lazing around at home then doing something productive no matter how much love for it they have.

I started to enjoy it more and more and as I got better, the people that would easily school me in the boxing ring were now having a hard time hitting me. My fitness improved dramatically and my obsession with learning the sport made me much better. I'd practice techniques in every spare moment I got. While walking, while driving, while showering, you name it. I now take personal training classes and have a healthy boxing routine that keeps me fit and improves my boxing skill at a faster than average pace. Hopefully I'll start competing sometime next year, (2016).

I don't have to force myself anymore. I love going to the boxing gym and getting better. Before I loved the thought of me being good at the sport but never really enjoyed the work that had to be put in. Now, I do.

All this from forcing myself for the first week or two. This is how motivation works. If you can't keep putting in effort when things aren't working out or you feel you're not getting anywhere with it then you'll just stop and quit. These are the moments you can't allow yourself to be a quitter. It may take a few days for you to see some results that will keep you going until you get what you want.

I've seen so many entrepreneurs who become successful at something explaining that it took them several attempts to finally see some decent results. For example, this kindle book is one of my very first books. I'm writing in hopes that I'll generate a decent monthly income from them.

I don't expect this one book to give me that result. Not that I think it's not good enough, it's more that business is a numbers game and you can never really grasp the potential of something until you give it a fair shot. I'm aiming to publish at least 20 or so books before I re-analyse to see if this business if for me. Will I be demotivated here and there throughout publishing those 20 books? Very likely, but as long as I understand that it's normal and you just have to keep going till you reach you're goal, I'll be ok and so will you if you understand this concept.

Negativity

Some people don't mean to be negative but that doesn't stop their words from having a negative impact on the way you think. One thing I've noticed being on this road is that it's incredibly lonely.

Don't get me wrong, I have a great friend circle and enjoy spending time with them but in terms of people understanding your thought processes and work activities, in most cases, you're on your own.

I remember when I first started internet marketing and I'd spend 10 hours+ days working at it in my room. I was so happy when I made my first sale of around $6 and couldn't help but to tell my family and friends about this amazing achievement. To me it was like striking gold for the first time with a pickaxe. To them, it was the silliest thing to be excited about and almost everyone had a dumbfounded, "really, is that it?" look on their face.

Every now and then someone would pull me aside and tell me that it might be a better option to go back to work. Use that degree I spent 4 years of my life getting. They meant the best for me but I didn't want that. I was making progress mentally and although had nothing to show for it at the time, I knew gains were being made.

Expect a lot of the above. Some people mean the best for you but they just don't know how to show it in these situations. Sometimes people seemingly close to you will actually be the most pessimistic towards your success. Either out of jealousy or complete doubt in your abilities in achieving it.

Take a break from these people if you need to. Connect yourself up to communities that keep you positive. Meetup groups, online forums, Skype groups, anywhere where you feel more at home. This is something that helped me greatly.

When I joined an affiliate marketing forum, everyone there were entrepreneurs and were used to facing all the challenges that I had. Many of them had gone on to make millions. It helped my mindset and kept me from dwelling on unnecessarily deconstructive thoughts.

Routines

I touched on this above but it's important so I thought I'd dedicate a whole section to it.

When you used to work full-time you had a set routine. When you began working for yourself whether it was part-time or full-time you're routine will begin to change.

You may have listened to a tonne of podcasts, read a lot of books and blog posts about the entrepreneur life and about the freedom it allows you to have with work hours. This all is true to an extent but routines are still required to achieve things.

Human beings can't function productively without them. You may not know it but already have routines for things that are mandatory in your life. From brushing your teeth to eating dinner. The time you do these activities is more or less set at a certain slot in the day or maybe even within a certain activity slot.

As you progress in your entrepreneurship career you'll begin to realise that in order to achieve your goal, you'll need to be consistent and that consistency can only come from making certain activities a 'routine' in your life.

When working or studying our routines are more or less handed to us. Someone, our superior, tutor, employer tells us when to start, when to stop, what to do and when to do it but when we're working for ourselves we have to make these on our own and stick to them. This is where the challenge lies.

I've experimented with a tonne of different routines. From sleeping 2 hours a day, (polyphasic sleep), to working on 4+ business ideas a day. Through trial and error I learned what works for me and gives me the most efficient output on a consistent basis.

You'll have to do the same. Not two entrepreneur routines are the same.

Some people enjoy the silence and serenity of the mornings where they wake up early and try and get as much un-interrupted work done as possible. Some enjoy this at night. Some people exercise first thing, some people like getting work done in the morning.

The start of your business life will be a lot of trial and error in everything. It's a huge adjustment and requires your time and patience. Three years later and I'm still adding/removing things from my routine.

Just know that every routine will require a healthy balance. Work, health, relationships will all need to be managed equally. Keep experimenting till you find what works for you and most importantly give yourself the time and headspace to achieve it.

The Real Entrepreneur Mindset

There's a massive difference between the way my mind works now and the way it used to work when I first stepped on the scene. For the most part, a quick comparison points out my naivety in being overly optimistic with my business ideas. Don't get me wrong, it's important to always be optimistic but with a half-baked plan you can't expect good results.

There are countless examples I can point to in my life where this has applied. All of my early ventures failed because I realised just how void they were of fundamental business principals.

For example, most of my ideas were great but I had no marketing plan. Telling friends and family by announcing your idea on FaceBook doesn't count as a marketing plan unfortunately. You might get some customers but it'll mostly be out of pity. You want to be able to make customers of people you've never met before. When you can do that, you've got yourself a healthy, stable business.

Another example is hopping to the next business idea too quickly. The fact is, it takes time for you to nut out the parts of your business model that need to be fine-tuned to a level where you start making money. This 'fine-tuning' takes time. Often months. If you're not willing to go at least a few months chasing your idea with consistent effort and proper marketing and sales then not only will you achieve nothing but you'll most likely learn nothing of value.

Trialling and testing takes time and these tests become more fruitful as your business matures. As you learn more, your business decisions are more in line with what they need to be and the frequency of them being successful will increase. You can't quit before you get to this level.

There are plenty of other things I can point out like proper dieting, the need to treat business like work not a hobby or 'side thing', etc. The bottom line is as you mature in your business career, your mindset will start to change. It's good but you may find yourself thinking way differently to most people around you. I've noticed most entrepreneurs think alike but there aren't many of us.

Business is Worth It

There are plenty of challenges that you'll face when heading down the entrepreneur road. These challenges will force you to grow and mature into someone not many people may be able to understand. There's a reason for that though. To get to a place where no one else is, you need to do things no one else does.

Business was the best decisions I ever made in my life. There were times I felt like crap, like going back, I doubted myself here and there but overall, the person I am now, able to create wealth out of nothing, not dependant on the countries economy, diversified and more secure with income, is a much better person.

If you're thinking about making the switch, there's a point where you'll just need to make a decision. Life will pass you by at an alarming rate the more routinely you allow it to get. Whether you're young or old, it doesn't matter. If you have the drive, you'll make it work. Anyone can do this, it just takes time to form the necessary habits and work ethics to make happen. The quicker you get started, the quicker you'll achieve your financial goals.

Lastly, I share part time business case studies and tips on entrepreneurship that have made me money to my Insider List.

Join Here ^   http://goo.gl/wcNCvW

Good luck!

Mateen S

Join Over 1,000 People in our Insider List

Insiders get Business Case Studies, Income Reports, the below upcoming Book Titles for free upon launch and much much more!

Join Here ^ *http://goo.gl/jQn9ou*

COMING SOON

Author Bio

Mateen has loved entrepreneurship since school. Buying and selling USB's, phones and game consoles on eBay and Gumtree, he learned the art of the hustle young.

Two years into his engineering career he quit to dedicate himself to entrepreneurship and take it to the next level.

Three years since the day he's quit from work life, he's made six figures from a variety of different entrepreneurship avenues. From selling merchandise on the famous Teespring platform to blogging. He's blog, affengineer.com, has been featured on prominent websites and is known to be the best for Teespring information.

He dedicates himself to finding ways to make money and sharing it with his insider list to create a community comfortable with sharing information and helping each other get to the financial place they desire.

www.ingramcontent.com/pod-product-compliance
Lightning Source LLC
Chambersburg PA
CBHW051226170526
45166CB00005B/2059